OH F*CK

NOT

ANOTHER

BIRTHDAY

summersdale

OH F*CK – NOT ANOTHER BIRTHDAY

An Hachette UK Company
www.hachette.co.uk

Summersdale Publishers Ltd
Part of Octopus Publishing Group Limited
Carmelite House
50 Victoria Embankment
LONDON
EC4Y 0DZ
UK

www.summersdale.com

Printed and bound in China

ISBN: 978-1-78783-266-4

Substantial discounts on bulk quantities of Summersdale books are available to corporations, professional associations and other organizations. For details contact general enquiries: telephone: +44 (0) 1243 771107 or email: enquiries@summersdale.com.

To.............................

From...........................

Why is a birthday cake
the only food you can
blow on and spit on
and everybody rushes
to get a piece?

BOBBY KELTON

YOU KNOW IT'S YOUR BIRTHDAY WHEN...

Your sock drawer goes from almost empty to bulging at the sides.

EAT CAKE AND
DRINK ENOUGH
TO FORGET
WHAT YOU'RE
CELEBRATING.

There is still
no cure for
the common
birthday.

JOHN GLENN

I feel I can talk with more authority, especially when I say, "I don't know."

**PETER USTINOV
ON GETTING OLDER**

YOU KNOW IT'S YOUR BIRTHDAY WHEN...

At the end of the day you're exhausted from all the attention you're not used to getting.

YOU'LL ALWAYS BE YOUNG ON THE INSIDE, RIGHT?

YOU KNOW YOU'RE GETTING OLDER WHEN THE CANDLES COST MORE THAN THE CAKE.

Bob Hope

Growing old
is compulsory.
Growing up
is optional.

BOB MONKHOUSE

YOU KNOW YOU'RE GETTING OLDER WHEN...

People congratulate
you for surviving
the year.

WHAT'S BETTER THAN A NIGHT OUT? A CANCELLED NIGHT OUT.

Birthdays are nature's way of telling you to eat more cake.

JO BRAND

THERE'S A VINTAGE
THAT COMES WITH AGE
AND EXPERIENCE.

JON BON JOVI

YOU KNOW YOU'RE GETTING OLDER WHEN...

Your bucket list is looking trickier to complete by the day.

HAPPY BIRTHDAY TO YOUR NEWEST WRINKLE.

The secret of
staying young is
to live honestly,
eat slowly and lie
about your age.

LUCILLE BALL

IF YOU WANT TO BE
ADORED BY YOUR
PEERS AND HAVE
STANDING OVATIONS
WHEREVER YOU GO –
LIVE TO BE OVER 90.

GEORGE ABBOTT

YOU KNOW IT'S YOUR BIRTHDAY WHEN...

People sing to you, and it still doesn't get any less awkward.

YOLO HAS BECOME YOOO (YOU'RE ONLY OLD ONCE).

Old age is not
for sissies.

BETTE DAVIS

I'm 59 and people call me middle-aged. How many 118-year-old men do you know?

BARRY CRYER

YOU KNOW YOU'RE GETTING OLDER WHEN...

You find another grey hair you hadn't noticed before.

GRIN AND BEAR IT.

YOU KNOW YOU'RE GETTING OLD WHEN EVERYTHING HURTS. AND WHAT DOESN'T HURT, DOESN'T WORK.

HY GARDNER

*Although I am 92,
my brain is
30 years old.*

ALFRED EISENSTAEDT

YOU KNOW YOU'RE GETTING OLDER WHEN...

You tell people not to get you anything and they take you seriously.

YOU'RE ALMOST
AT THE TOP OF
THE HILL... AT
LEAST YOU'RE
NOT BURIED
BENEATH IT.

Anyone can get old. All you have to do is live long enough.

GROUCHO MARX

EVENTUALLY YOU WILL
REACH A POINT WHEN
YOU STOP LYING ABOUT
YOUR AGE AND START
BRAGGING ABOUT IT.

WILL ROGERS

YOU KNOW IT'S YOUR BIRTHDAY WHEN...

Everyone's treating you like a rare and valuable fossil.

A LITTLE AGE ADDS A LOT OF FLAVOUR.

I've really had to
come to terms
with the fact I
am now a walking
and talking adult.

MATT DILLON

I DO WISH I COULD
TELL YOU MY AGE
BUT IT'S IMPOSSIBLE.
IT KEEPS CHANGING
ALL THE TIME.

GREER GARSON

YOU KNOW IT'S YOUR BIRTHDAY WHEN...

You remember your age... and then wish the memory loss would set in.

THANKFULLY YOU ONLY HAVE ONE BIRTHDAY A YEAR. FOR THE OTHER 364 DAYS YOU CAN CARRY ON LIKE NOTHING'S CHANGED.

Old age is the outpatients' department of purgatory.

HUGH CECIL

How foolish to think that one can ever slam the door in the face of age. Much wiser to be polite and gracious and ask him to lunch in advance.

NOËL COWARD

YOU KNOW YOU'RE GETTING OLDER WHEN...

Your bathroom looks like a health and beauty store.

BACK IN MY DAY I WAS NEVER THIS OLD.

Old people shouldn't
eat health foods.
They need all
the preservatives
they can get.

ROBERT ORBEN

Youth is like spring, an overpraised season.

SAMUEL BUTLER

YOU KNOW IT'S YOUR BIRTHDAY WHEN...

People keep lighting your food on fire.

A MOMENT ON THE LIPS, A LIFETIME ON YOUR SURGICALLY REPAIRED HIPS.

Why am I getting older and wider instead of older and wiser?

ANONYMOUS

AGE IS STRICTLY A CASE
OF MIND OVER MATTER.
IF YOU DON'T MIND,
IT DOESN'T MATTER.

JACK BENNY

YOU KNOW IT'S YOUR BIRTHDAY WHEN...

You dread going into work in case the word has spread.

CONGRATULATIONS! YOU'VE SURVIVED ANOTHER YEAR.

*The idea is to die
young as late
as possible.*

ASHLEY MONTAGU

Age is a very high price to pay for maturity.

TOM STOPPARD

YOU KNOW IT'S YOUR BIRTHDAY WHEN...

You don't have to feel guilty about overindulging, overspending, oversleeping...

YOUNG AT HEART... SLIGHTLY OLDER IN OTHER PLACES.

To me, old age is always 15 years older than I am.

BERNARD BARUCH

AGE IS SOMETHING THAT DOESN'T MATTER, UNLESS YOU ARE A CHEESE.

BILLIE BURKE

YOU KNOW YOU'RE GETTING OLDER WHEN...

You have to stop yourself from selling your unwanted presents until at least the next day.

I AM NOT AGEING;
I AM INCREASING
IN VALUE.

Anonymous

AT LEAST YOU'RE NOT AS OLD AS YOU WILL BE NEXT YEAR!

**Inside every
older person is
a younger person
wondering what
the hell happened.**

CORA HARVEY ARMSTRONG

YOU KNOW YOU'RE GETTING OLDER WHEN...

You're scared to smile in case your teeth fall out.

TOO MANY BIRTHDAYS CAN KILL YOU.

YOU'RE IN PRETTY GOOD SHAPE FOR THE SHAPE YOU ARE IN!

Dr Seuss

Old age isn't so bad when you consider the alternative.

MAURICE CHEVALIER

YOU KNOW IT'S YOUR BIRTHDAY WHEN...

You wish people would stop reminding you how old you are.

YOU LOOK GREAT... FOR YOUR AGE.

WISDOM DOESN'T
NECESSARILY COME
WITH AGE. SOMETIMES
AGE JUST SHOWS UP
ALL BY ITSELF.

TOM WILSON

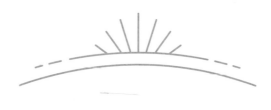

YOUTH WOULD BE
AN IDEAL STATE IF
IT CAME A LITTLE
LATER IN LIFE.

H. H. ASQUITH

YOU KNOW IT'S YOUR BIRTHDAY WHEN...

You are greeted
by brightly coloured
envelopes instead of bills.

HAVE A HAPPY F*CKING BIRTHDAY.

I'm at an age
when my back
goes out more
than I do.

PHYLLIS DILLER

One trouble with growing older is that it gets progressively tougher to find a famous historical figure who didn't amount to much when he was your age.

BILL VAUGHAN

YOU KNOW IT'S YOUR BIRTHDAY WHEN...

You're treated like royalty for one day and one day only.

A BIRTHDAY
A YEAR?
THERE'S
NOTHING
TO FEAR.

It takes a very
long time to
become young.

PABLO PICASSO

MIDDLE AGE IS
WHEN YOUR AGE
STARTS TO SHOW
AROUND YOUR MIDDLE.

BOB HOPE

YOU KNOW YOU'RE GETTING OLDER WHEN...

Your cake starts to resemble a porcupine.

THE OLDER YOU ARE, THE EARLIER IT GETS LATE.

To what do I
attribute my
longevity? Bad
luck, mostly.

BILLY WILDER

LIFE WAS A FUNNY
THING THAT HAPPENED
TO ME ON THE WAY
TO THE GRAVE.

QUENTIN CRISP

YOU KNOW IT'S YOUR BIRTHDAY WHEN...

You don't feel any guilt about wolfing down multiple slices of cake.

One great thing about getting old is that you can get out of all sorts of social obligations just by saying you're tired.

GEORGE CARLIN

I'M NOT GETTING OLD. I'M JUST BECOMING A CLASSIC.

I think all this talk about age is foolish. Every time I'm one year older, everyone else is too.

GLORIA SWANSON

YOU KNOW YOU'RE GETTING OLDER WHEN...

You're beyond the point of caring about getting old. That ship sailed a long, long time ago.

A BIRTHDAY IS A CELEBRATION FOR THE YOUNG AND A NUISANCE FOR THE OLD.

All that I know
I learned after
I was 30.

GEORGES CLEMENCEAU

Please don't retouch my wrinkles. It took me so long to earn them.

ANNA MAGNANI

YOU KNOW YOU'RE GETTING OLDER WHEN...

Your real friends
remember the day
but not your age.

LIVE YOUR LIFE AND FORGET YOUR AGE.

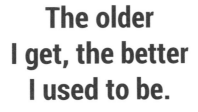

The older I get, the better I used to be.

LEE TREVINO

OLD AGE IS LIKE
LEARNING A NEW
PROFESSION. AND
NOT ONE OF YOUR
OWN CHOOSING.

JACQUES BARZUN

YOU KNOW IT'S YOUR BIRTHDAY WHEN...

You get reminded that age is just a number. A big, fat, ever-increasing number.

A PARTY
WITHOUT
CAKE IS
JUST A
MEETING.

I have everything
I had 20 years ago,
only it's all a
little bit lower.

GYPSY ROSE LEE

They tell you that you'll lose your mind when you grow older. What they don't tell you is that you won't miss it very much.

MALCOLM COWLEY

YOU KNOW YOU'RE GETTING OLDER WHEN...

Happy hour is nap time.

**NOTHING SAYS
HAPPY BIRTHDAY
LIKE A PIECE OF
FOLDED CARD.**

The seven ages of man: spills, drills, thrills, bills, ills, pills and wills.

RICHARD J. NEEDHAM

I can honestly
say I love getting
older. Then again,
I never put my
glasses on before
looking in the mirror.

CHERIE LUNGHI

YOU KNOW YOU'RE GETTING OLDER WHEN...

The latest music
sounds as melodic
as a drill.

IF THE GOOD
OLD DAYS HAVE
PASSED, WHAT
DAYS ARE WE IN
NOW: THE CRAP
NEW ONES?

WHEN I WAS A BOY, THE DEAD SEA WAS ONLY SICK.

George Burns

YOU KNOW YOU'RE GETTING OLDER WHEN...

People begin to tell you how good you look for your age.

IF I KNEW THAT I
WAS GOING TO LIVE
THIS LONG, I'D HAVE
TAKEN BETTER
CARE OF MYSELF.

MICKEY MANTLE

PEOPLE CAN'T
SAY YOU ARE
WISE BEYOND
YOUR YEARS
ANYMORE.

YOUTH IS WHEN YOU'RE ALLOWED TO STAY UP LATE ON NEW YEAR'S EVE. MIDDLE AGE IS WHEN YOU'RE FORCED TO.

Bill Vaughan

IN ONE OLD PEOPLE'S HOME THEY CHANGED THE WORDS OF THE SONG TO "WHEN I'M 84" AS THEY CONSIDERED 64 TO BE YOUNG.

PAUL McCARTNEY

YOU KNOW YOU'RE GETTING OLDER WHEN...

You gain a new party trick: being able to cough, sneeze and pee yourself at the same time!

WHEN LIFE GIVES YOU A BIRTHDAY, EAT CAKE.

GROWING OLD IS LIKE
BEING INCREASINGLY
PENALIZED FOR A
CRIME YOU HAVEN'T
COMMITTED.

ANTHONY POWELL

*I intend to live forever.
So far, so good.*

STEVEN WRIGHT

YOU KNOW IT'S YOUR BIRTHDAY WHEN...

Your main achievement
is that you've made
a full trip around the
sun once again.

NOW WHERE DID I PUT MY KEYS?

ONE SHOULD NEVER
MAKE ONE'S DEBUT
WITH A SCANDAL. ONE
SHOULD RESERVE THAT
TO GIVE AN INTEREST
TO ONE'S OLD AGE.

OSCAR WILDE

ONE OF THE BEST
PARTS OF GROWING
OLDER? YOU CAN FLIRT
ALL YOU LIKE SINCE
YOU'VE BECOME
HARMLESS.

LIZ SMITH

YOU KNOW YOU'RE GETTING OLDER WHEN...

You don't need to be worried about getting tooth rot from too much sugar any more. All your teeth are fake.

YOUR BIRTHDAY CAKES ARE BECOMING A SERIOUS FIRE HAZARD.

OLD AGE: WHEN ACTIONS CREAK LOUDER THAN WORDS.

Dana Robbins

If you survive long enough, you're revered – rather like an old building.

KATHARINE HEPBURN

YOU KNOW YOU'RE GETTING OLDER WHEN...

You get birthday texts rather than calls. Kids and their technology these days...

THE OLDER YOU GET, THE EARLIER YOU'RE HOME AND READY FOR BED.

How do I confront ageing? With a wonder and a terror.

KEANU REEVES

Your life is written on your face.

FRANCES McDORMAND

YOU KNOW YOU'RE GETTING OLDER WHEN...

You wake up after the celebrations and realize your alcohol tolerance isn't what it used to be.

WHEN WILL THE TEENAGE ANGST WEAR OFF?

There's one
more terrifying
fact about old
people: I'm going
to be one soon.

P. J. O'ROURKE

YOU KNOW IT'S YOUR BIRTHDAY WHEN...

Everyone is being suspiciously nice to you and it takes you a while to figure out why.

THE AGEING PROCESS
HAS YOU FIRMLY IN ITS
GRASP IF YOU NEVER
GET THE URGE TO
THROW A SNOWBALL.

DOUG LARSON

BIRTHDAY?
WHOSE
BIRTHDAY?

The way I see
it, you should live
every day like it's
your birthday.

PARIS HILTON

Inflation is when you pay fifteen dollars for the ten-dollar haircut you used to get for five dollars when you had hair.

SAM EWING

YOU KNOW YOU'RE GETTING OLDER WHEN...

People start referring
to you as vintage
and mean it as a
compliment.

AT LEAST
EVERYONE
YOUR AGE
IS OLDER
THAN YOU.

THEY SAY THAT AGE
IS ALL IN YOUR MIND.
THE TRICK IS KEEPING
IT FROM CREEPING
DOWN INTO YOUR BODY.

ANONYMOUS

THE FIRST SIGN OF
MATURITY IS THE
DISCOVERY THAT THE
VOLUME KNOB ALSO
TURNS TO THE LEFT.

JERRY M. WRIGHT

YOU KNOW IT'S YOUR BIRTHDAY WHEN...

You have your happy-surprised face for present opening down to a tee.

The key to successful ageing is to pay as little attention to it as possible.

JUDITH REGAN

LIFE'S TOO SHORT. EVEN SHORTER NOW.

Middle age is when your broad mind and narrow waist begin to change places.

E. JOSEPH COSSMAN

YOU KNOW IT'S YOUR BIRTHDAY WHEN...

You are contacted by distant relatives who you haven't seen for years.

WHAT IS IT
THEY SAY ABOUT
GETTING OLDER
AGAIN? YEAH,
I DON'T
REMEMBER
EITHER.

I PLAN ON GROWING OLD MUCH LATER IN LIFE, OR MAYBE NOT AT ALL.

Patty Carey

YOUNG PEOPLE
DON'T KNOW WHAT AGE IS,
AND OLD PEOPLE FORGET
WHAT YOUTH WAS.

IRISH PROVERB

YOU KNOW YOU'RE GETTING OLDER WHEN...

People you haven't seen in years begin to reminisce about the "good old days".

YOUR YOUNGER
SELF WOULD
PROBABLY HATE
WHAT YOU'VE
BECOME. BUT
THAT PERSON
WAS A FOOL, SO
WHO CARES?

Age is just a number and mine is unlisted.

ANONYMOUS

THE GREAT THING ABOUT GETTING OLDER IS THAT YOU DON'T LOSE ALL THE OTHER AGES YOU'VE BEEN.

MADELEINE L'ENGLE

YOU KNOW YOU'RE GETTING OLDER WHEN...

You reply,
"old enough" if
someone asks how
old you are.

THE TIME TO START LYING ABOUT YOUR AGE WAS A GOOD TEN YEARS AGO.

Anticipate the day as if it was your birthday and you are turning six again.

MIKE DOLAN

I don't so much mind being old, as I mind being fat and old.

PETER GABRIEL

YOU KNOW IT'S YOUR BIRTHDAY WHEN...

Midweek drinking
is excused.

PLEASE DO NOT REMIND ME WHAT DAY IT IS.

It used to be that
my age and waist
size were the same.
Unfortunately,
they still are.

ANONYMOUS

The older you get
the stronger the
wind gets – and it's
always in your face.

JACK NICKLAUS

YOU KNOW YOU'RE GETTING OLDER WHEN...

The songs of
your youth are now
considered "classics".

DON'T LET AGEING GET YOU DOWN. IT'S TOO HARD TO GET BACK UP.

JOHN WAGNER

OH F*CK – NOT ANOTHER BIRTHDAY!

If you're interested in finding out more about our books, find us on Facebook at Summersdale Publishers and follow us on Twitter at @Summersdale.

www.summersdale.com

Image credits

Straight and curved scroll details – pp.1, 3, 5, 8, 9, 13, 16, 17, 20, 21, 25, 27, 29, 32, 33, 36, 37, 41, 45, 48, 49, 51, 53, 56, 57, 61, 65, 67, 68, 69, 73, 75, 76, 77, 80, 81, 85, 89, 93, 97, 99, 101, 104, 105, 108, 109, 111, 112, 113, 116, 117, 121, 125, 128, 129, 133, 136, 137, 141, 145, 147, 148, 149, 152, 158, 157
© Ezepov Dmitry/Shutterstock.com